W9-BFB-965

FAVORITE BRAND NAME

GREAT GARLIC RECIPES

Publications International, Ltd.

Copyright © 1997 Publications International, Ltd.
All rights reserved. This publication may not be reproduced or quoted in whole or in part by any means whatsoever without written permission from:

Louis Weber, CEO
Publications International, Ltd.
7373 North Cicero Avenue
Lincolnwood, Illinois 60646

Permission is never granted for commercial purposes.

All recipes and photographs that contain specific brand names are copyrighted by those companies and/or associations, unless otherwise specified. All photographs *except* those on pages 58 and 83 copyright © Publications International, Ltd.

Some of the products listed in this publication may be in limited distribution.

Front cover photography and photography on pages 7, 9, 17, 29, 39, 49, 63 and 73 by Stephen Hamilton Photographics.

Pictured on the front cover: Forty Clove Chicken *(page 59).*

Pictured on the back cover *(from top):* Tenderloin with Roasted Garlic Sauce *(page 72),* Baked Shrimp with Chili-Garlic Butter *(page 62)* and Sweet Pepper Garlic Soup *(page 16).*

ISBN: 0-7853-2459-3

Manufactured in U.S.A.

8 7 6 5 4 3 2 1

Microwave Cooking: Microwave ovens vary in wattage. Use the cooking times as guidelines and check for doneness before adding more time.

FAVORITE BRAND NAME

GREAT GARLIC RECIPES

■ Introduction 6 ■

■ Appetizers 8 ■

■ Soups & Salads 16 ■

■ Vegetables & Sides 28 ■

■ Pasta 38 ■

■ Poultry 48 ■

■ Seafood 62 ■

■ Beef, Lamb & Pork 72 ■

■ Acknowledgments 92 ■

■ Index 93 ■

INTRODUCTION

Throughout history, this wonderful little bulb has been hailed for its flavor, pungency and healing powers. Garlic was believed to give courage and strength, to cure diseases such as consumption and influenza and to ward off vampires. Recent studies have shown that eating generous amounts of garlic may play a role in protecting against heart disease. Results indicate that garlic may cause serum cholesterol levels to drop, help prevent blood clots that lead to heart attacks and strokes and aid in lowering blood pressure.

Garlic has been popular for centuries for more than its medicinal qualities! It has found its way into the hearts of millions of people around the world because of its exceptional flavor and versatility. Garlic is a staple in Italian, Chinese, Mexican, Thai and Mediterranean cuisines, just to name a few. Garlic is the star ingredient of buttery shrimp scampi, hearty bowls of chili and crisp Caesar salads.

Garlic Know-How

Although there are many varieties of garlic, most have the same characteristic pungent odor and bite and can be used interchangeably in recipes. The most common variety of garlic is American garlic, which has white skin and a strong flavor. Mexican and Italian garlic are pink skinned and taste sweeter. Elephant garlic, with its large cloves, is very mild.

When purchasing garlic, look for heads that are plump, firm to the touch and have no visible damp or brown spots. Garlic will keep anywhere from a few weeks to a few months depending on its age and how it is stored at home. For best results, garlic should be stored in a cool, dark, dry spot.

The whole garlic bulb is called a head. Each individual section is called a clove. Peeling a clove of garlic is very simple—just trim off ends and slightly crush cloves with the flat side of a large knife. The pressure of the knife separates the skin from the clove.

There is no need to peel garlic if you are using a garlic press. The garlic gets passed through the press leaving the skin behind. Since pressing garlic releases more of its essential oils, it can be as much as 10 times stronger in flavor as sliced or whole garlic. Keep this in mind when deciding on how much garlic flavor you want in your dish. Don't forget to thoroughly wash your garlic press after each use. The oils left behind in the press can quickly turn rancid and pass an off flavor the next time the press is used.

Roasting garlic produces a mild, sweet, nutty flavor. Because it is milder, roasted garlic can be used more liberally than raw garlic.

To roast garlic, simply cut off the top third of the garlic head (not the root end) to expose the cloves; discard the top. Place the head of garlic, trimmed end up, on a 10-inch square of foil. Rub the head generously with olive oil and sprinkle it with salt. Gather the foil ends together and close tightly. Roast in a preheated 350°F oven 45 minutes or until cloves are golden and the head is soft.

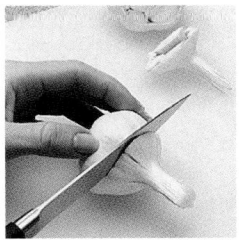

Set aside until cool enough to handle. Gently squeeze the softened garlic head from the root end toward the cut end so that the roasted cloves slip out of their skins into a small bowl. Discard the skins.

Mash the cloves with a fork and use in your favorite recipe. It can also be spread on warm French bread, whipped into mashed potatoes, blended into marinara sauce or used as a sandwich spread. Its uses are endless!

APPETIZERS

Roasted ■ Eggplant Dip ■

2 eggplants (about 1 pound each)
3 tablespoons sesame tahini*
¼ cup lemon juice
4 cloves garlic, minced
2 teaspoons hot pepper sauce
½ teaspoon salt
Paprika
1 tablespoon chopped fresh parsley

**Available in the ethnic section of the supermarket or in Middle Eastern grocery stores.*

1. Prick eggplants in several places with fork. To roast over charcoal, place eggplants on grill over hot coals; cook about 30 to 40 minutes or until skin is black and blistered and pulp is soft, turning often. To roast in oven, preheat oven to 450°F. Place eggplants on baking sheet; bake about 30 to 40 minutes or until skin is blistered and pulp is soft.

2. Peel eggplants when cool enough to handle. Let cool to room temperature.

3. Place eggplant pulp in food processor with tahini, lemon juice, garlic, hot pepper sauce and salt; process until smooth. Refrigerate at least 1 hour before serving to allow flavors to blend. Sprinkle dip with paprika and parsley; serve with pita bread wedges. Garnish with red chili pepper slices, if desired.

Makes 8 servings

Roasted Eggplant Dip

Herbed Garlic ■ Cheese Spread ■

1 cup (8 ounces) low-fat or non-fat cottage cheese
¼ cup roasted garlic (page 7)
1 cup (4 ounces) shredded JARLSBERG Cheese or JARLSBERG LITE™ Cheese
½ teaspoon dried tarragon
¼ teaspoon freshly ground black pepper

Place cottage cheese in blender with roasted garlic and blend well. Add Jarlsberg and tarragon. Blend, scraping down sides (mixture will be slightly lumpy). Add pepper; stir and taste. Add more pepper, if desired. Serve with carrot or zucchini rounds, red pepper strips and celery sticks.

Makes 1½ cups

Note: Spread may be served warm. Microwave on high 1½ minutes, stirring every 30 seconds or cook in double boiler, stirring over simmering water until warm.

Marshall's Garlic ■ Popcorn ■

10 to 12 cloves garlic, thinly sliced
4 to 5 tablespoons vegetable oil
½ cup NEWMAN'S OWN® Oldstyle Picture Show Popcorn
1 tablespoon butter
Garlic salt
Parmesan cheese (optional)

Rub garlic slices over bottom of an electric (oil) corn popper. Cook and stir garlic slices with oil in small skillet until golden brown. Drain to remove the garlic slices, reserving oil and garlic separately. Pour the oil into the corn popper. Add NEWMAN'S OWN® Oldstyle Picture Show Popcorn and pop as usual. Melt butter; combine with reserved garlic. After the popping is completed, place popcorn in serving bowl. Toss with garlic butter; season with garlic salt and Parmesan cheese, if desired.

Makes 4 servings

■ Garlic Bites ■

½ of 16-ounce package frozen phyllo dough, thawed to room temperature
¾ cup butter, melted
3 large heads garlic, separated into cloves, peeled
½ cup finely chopped walnuts
1 cup Italian-style bread crumbs

Preheat oven to 350°F. Remove phyllo from package; unroll and place on large sheet of waxed paper. Cut phyllo crosswise into 2-inch-wide strips. Cover phyllo with large sheet of plastic wrap and damp, clean kitchen towel. (Phyllo dries out quickly if not covered.)

Lay 1 strip of phyllo at a time on flat surface and brush immediately with melted butter. Place 1 clove of garlic at end. Sprinkle 1 teaspoon walnuts along length of strip.

Roll up garlic clove and walnuts in strip, tucking in side edges as you roll. Brush Garlic Bite with more butter. Roll in bread crumbs. Repeat with remaining phyllo, garlic, walnuts and butter.

Place Garlic Bites on rack in shallow roasting pan. Bake 20 minutes.

Makes 24 to 27 appetizers

Garlic Bites

■ Garlic Fritters ■

10 large cloves CHRISTOPHER RANCH Fresh Garlic, finely chopped
¼ teaspoon salt
1 cup water
6 tablespoons butter
1 cup all-purpose flour
4 eggs
Oil for deep-frying
¼ cup sour cream
¼ cup grated Parmesan cheese
2 cloves CHRISTOPHER RANCH Fresh Garlic, minced
2 teaspoons chopped fresh tarragon *or* 1 teaspoon dried tarragon

Combine finely chopped garlic and salt in small bowl; mash into a paste. Combine water, garlic paste and butter in saucepan over medium heat; bring to a boil. Add flour, stirring quickly into a mass. Remove from heat. Add eggs, 1 at a time, being certain to fully incorporate each one. Form dough into small bite-sized mounds and deep-fry at about 370°F until golden brown. Drain on paper towels. Cut each fritter in half. Combine sour cream, Parmesan, minced garlic and tarragon in small bowl. Spread ½ teaspoon of sour cream mixture on half of each fritter; top with other half. *Makes 4 dozen appetizers*

Roasted Garlic ■ Hummus ■

1 can (15 ounces) chick-peas, rinsed and drained
¼ cup fresh parsley, stems removed
2 tablespoons roasted garlic (page 7)
2 tablespoons lemon juice
2 tablespoons water
½ teaspoon curry powder
3 drops dark sesame oil
Dash hot pepper sauce

Place chick-peas, parsley, roasted garlic, lemon juice, water, curry powder, sesame oil and hot pepper sauce in food processor or blender; process until smooth, scraping down side of bowl once. Serve with pita bread triangles or crackers.

Makes 6 servings

Fiery Garlic ■ Bagel Thins ■

5 bagels
½ cup (1 stick) butter
6 cloves garlic, minced
2 tablespoons lemon juice
½ teaspoon TABASCO® pepper sauce
Salt to taste

Preheat broiler. Slice bagels crosswise into fifths. Melt butter in a small saucepan. Add garlic; cook over low heat for 2 minutes or until garlic has softened. Add lemon juice, TABASCO® sauce and salt to taste. Liberally brush one side of each bagel slice with lemon-garlic butter. Broil bagels on one side until golden. Watch carefully; this only takes a minute. Turn bagels over and broil until golden. Serve hot or store in an airtight container.

Makes 25 bagel thins

■ Salsa Cruda ■

1 cup chopped tomato
2 tablespoons minced onion
2 tablespoons minced fresh cilantro
2 tablespoons lime juice
½ jalapeño pepper,* seeded and minced
3 cloves garlic, minced

**Jalapeño peppers can sting and irritate the skin; wear rubber gloves when handling peppers and do not touch eyes. Wash hands after handling.*

Combine all ingredients in small bowl; mix well. Serve with tortilla chips.

Makes 4 servings

■ Stuffed Mushrooms ■

12 large mushrooms
2 tablespoons butter or margarine
3 cloves CHRISTOPHER RANCH Elephant Garlic, chopped
3 shallots, chopped
⅔ cup shredded Swiss cheese
⅓ cup dry bread crumbs
Parmesan cheese for garnish

Remove stems from mushrooms; chop stems and reserve caps. Melt butter in medium skillet over medium heat. Add chopped mushroom stems, garlic and shallots; cook and stir until garlic and shallots are soft. Remove from heat; stir in Swiss cheese and bread crumbs. Stuff the mushroom caps full and place in baking dish. Bake in a 375°F oven for 15 to 20 minutes. Sprinkle each with Parmesan before serving.

Makes 4 to 6 servings

■ Venezuelan Salsa ■

1 carrot, finely chopped
1 small onion, finely chopped
1 rib celery, finely chopped
1 mango, peeled, pitted and diced
½ medium papaya, peeled, seeded and diced
½ medium avocado, peeled, pitted and diced
Juice of 1 lemon
3 cloves garlic, minced
1 jalapeño pepper,* finely chopped
1½ teaspoons ground cumin
½ teaspoon salt
2 tablespoons chopped cilantro

**Jalapeño peppers can sting and irritate the skin; wear rubber gloves when handling peppers and do not touch eyes. Wash hands after handling.*

Combine all ingredients in medium bowl. Refrigerate several hours to allow flavors to blend. Serve with tortilla chips, carrot and celery sticks or apple wedges.

Makes 10 servings (¼ cup each)

■ Elephant in a Bowl ■

1 package (8 ounces) cream cheese, softened
1 cup shredded Monterey Jack or Swiss cheese
¼ cup diced mild green chilies
3 cloves CHRISTOPHER RANCH Elephant Garlic, finely chopped
2 tablespoons finely chopped fresh parsley
Pinch of white pepper
1 large round French bread loaf

Preheat oven to 350°F. Combine cream cheese, Monterey Jack, chilies, garlic, parsley and white pepper in large bowl; blend well. Slice off top of French bread and scoop out enough bread to create a bowl to comfortably hold cheese mixture. Place cheese mixture into bread bowl and replace top. Wrap in foil; bake for 20 to 30 minutes or until heated through. Serve with crackers or French bread slices.

Makes 8 to 10 servings

Venezuelan Salsa

Soups & Salads

Sweet Pepper Garlic ■ Soup ■

2 teaspoons olive oil
½ cup chopped onion
6 cloves garlic, chopped
3½ cups chicken broth
1 cup cubed potato, unpeeled
1 cup chopped red bell pepper
1 cup cottage cheese
2 tablespoons plain yogurt
⅛ teaspoon black pepper

1. Heat oil in medium saucepan over medium heat; add onion and garlic. Cook and stir 3 minutes or until onion is tender. Add chicken broth, potato and bell pepper. Bring to a boil; reduce heat and simmer 10 to 15 minutes or until potato is easily pierced when tested with fork. Remove from heat; cool completely.

2. Place broth mixture in food processor or blender; process until smooth. Refrigerate until completely cool.

3. Place cottage cheese and yogurt in food processor or blender; process until smooth. Set aside ¼ cup cheese mixture. Stir remaining cheese mixture into chilled broth mixture until well blended. Add black pepper; stir well. Top with reserved cheese mixture. Garnish with parsley and bell pepper strips, if desired.

Makes 6 servings

Sweet Pepper Garlic Soup

Albacore Salad Puttanesca with Garlic ■ Vinaigrette ■

- 2 cups cooked, chilled angel hair pasta
- 2 cups chopped, peeled plum tomatoes
- 1 can (4¼ ounces) chopped black olives, drained
- 1 cup Garlic Vinaigrette Dressing (recipe follows)
- 1 can (6 ounces) STARKIST® Solid White Tuna, drained and flaked
- ¼ cup chopped fresh basil leaves

In large bowl, combine chilled pasta, tomatoes, olives and Garlic Vinaigrette Dressing. Add tuna and basil leaves; toss. Serve immediately. *Makes 2 servings*

Garlic Vinaigrette Dressing

- ⅓ cup red wine vinegar
- 2 tablespoons lemon juice
- 1 to 2 cloves garlic, minced or pressed
- 1 teaspoon black pepper
- Salt
- 1 cup olive oil

In small bowl, whisk together vinegar, lemon juice, garlic, pepper and salt to taste. Slowly add oil, whisking continuously, until well blended. *Makes about 1⅓ cups*

Mexican Tortilla ■ Soup ■

- 1 tablespoon vegetable oil
- 1 rib celery, sliced
- ½ cup sliced carrots
- 3 green onions, sliced
- 4 cloves garlic, minced
- 2 cans (about 14 ounces each) chicken broth
- ⅓ to ½ cup lime juice
- Baked Tortilla Strips (page 21)
- ½ cup chopped tomato
- ½ small avocado, chopped
- ¼ cup chopped seeded cucumber
- 2 tablespoons finely chopped fresh cilantro

Heat oil in medium saucepan over medium heat. Add celery, carrots, green onions and garlic; cook and stir about 5 minutes or until tender. Add chicken broth and lime juice; bring to a boil over high heat. Reduce heat to low; simmer, covered, 15 minutes. Meanwhile, prepare Baked Tortilla Strips.

Ladle soup into 4 bowls; divide tomato, avocado and cucumber among bowls. Sprinkle with cilantro and tortilla strips. Serve immediately. *Makes 4 servings*

Albacore Salad Puttanesca with Garlic Vinaigrette

Grilled Summer ■ Gazpacho ■

1 red bell pepper, stemmed, seeded and halved
4 large (about 2 pounds) tomatoes, tops removed
1 small onion, halved
Nonstick cooking spray
4 cloves garlic, divided
6 (½-inch) slices French bread
1 cup coarsely chopped peeled cucumber
1 cup day-old French bread cubes, soaked in water and squeezed dry
2 to 4 tablespoons chopped fresh cilantro
2 tablespoons lemon juice
1 tablespoon olive oil
½ teaspoon salt
2 cups ice water
Additional cilantro leaves for garnish

1. Prepare coals for grilling. Grill bell pepper halves, skin side down, on covered grill over medium to hot coals 15 to 25 minutes or until skin is charred, without turning. Remove from grill and place in plastic bag until cool enough to handle, about 10 minutes. Remove skin; set peppers aside to cool.

2. Meanwhile, spray tomatoes and onion halves with cooking spray. Grill tomatoes and onion halves, skin side down, on covered grill over medium coals 10 to 20 minutes or until grillmarked and tender, turning as needed. Thread 3 garlic cloves onto water-soaked wooden or bamboo skewer. Spray with cooking spray. Grill garlic on covered grill over medium coals about 8 minutes or until browned and tender. Remove vegetables from grill and let cool on cutting board.

3. While vegetables cool, cut remaining garlic clove in half. Spray both sides of French bread slices with cooking spray; rub with garlic clove halves. Grill bread slices on both sides until toasted and golden, watching carefully. Cool; cut into ½-inch croutons and set aside for garnish.

4. Gently squeeze cooled tomatoes to remove seeds and release skins. Scrape and discard any excess charring from onion. Coarsely chop bell pepper, tomatoes and onion; add with cucumber to food processor or blender. Cover and process until smooth. Transfer to large bowl.

5. Add soaked bread cubes, chopped cilantro, lemon juice, oil and salt to food processor; cover and process until smooth. Combine with grilled vegetable mixture; stir in ice water. Ladle soup into bowls; garnish with garlic croutons and additional cilantro leaves, if desired. *Makes 6 servings*

■ Taos Tossed Salad ■

Baked Tortilla Strips (recipe follows)
¼ cup orange juice
1 tablespoon white wine vinegar
1 teaspoon olive oil
4 cloves garlic, minced
¼ teaspoon ground cumin
¼ teaspoon black pepper
3 cups washed and torn romaine leaves
1 cup washed and torn Boston lettuce leaves
1 cup julienned jicama
2 medium oranges, cut into segments
1 medium tomato, cut into wedges
¼ cup thinly sliced red onion

Prepare Baked Tortilla Strips; set aside.

For dressing, combine orange juice, vinegar, oil, garlic, cumin and pepper in small jar with tight-fitting lid; shake well. Refrigerate until ready to use.

Combine lettuces, jicama, oranges, tomato and onion in large bowl. Shake dressing; pour over salad and toss gently to coat. Sprinkle with Baked Tortilla Strips. Serve immediately. *Makes 6 servings*

Baked Tortilla Strips

2 (6-inch) flour tortillas
Nonstick cooking spray
Dash paprika

Preheat oven to 375°F. Cut tortillas into halves; cut halves into ¼-inch-wide strips. Arrange tortilla strips on cookie sheet. Spray lightly with cooking spray; toss to coat. Sprinkle with paprika.

Bake about 10 minutes or until browned, stirring occasionally. Let cool to room temperature.

Makes about 1½ cups

Layered Mexican ■ Salad ■

- 1 small head romaine lettuce
- Salsa Cruda (page 13)
- 1 can (15 ounces) black turtle beans, rinsed and drained
- 1 cup frozen corn, thawed and drained
- 1 large cucumber, peeled
- 1 can (2¼ ounces) sliced black olives, drained
- 1 large lemon
- ¾ cup mayonnaise
- 3 tablespoons plain yogurt
- 4 cloves garlic, minced
- ½ cup (2 ounces) shredded Cheddar cheese
- 1 green onion, thinly sliced

1. Cut romaine leaves crosswise into ½-inch strips; place half in large serving bowl. Layer with Salsa Cruda, beans and corn.

2. Halve cucumber lengthwise; scoop out and discard seeds. Slice thinly. Place cucumber over corn, sprinkle with olives and top with remaining lettuce.

3. Grate lemon peel; combine with mayonnaise, yogurt and garlic. Juice lemon; stir 3 to 4 tablespoons juice into dressing. Spread dressing evenly over top of salad. Sprinkle with cheese and green onion. Cover; refrigerate 2 hours or up to 1 day.

Makes 12 servings

■ Far East Tabbouleh ■

- ¾ cup uncooked bulgur
- 2 tablespoons teriyaki sauce
- 2 tablespoons lemon juice
- 1 tablespoon olive oil
- ¾ cup diced seeded cucumber
- ¾ cup diced seeded tomato
- ½ cup thinly sliced green onions
- ½ cup minced fresh cilantro or fresh parsley
- 1 tablespoon minced fresh ginger
- 4 cloves garlic, crushed

1. Combine bulgur and 1¾ cups boiling water in small bowl. Cover with plastic wrap; let stand 45 minutes or until bulgur is puffed, stirring occasionally. Drain in wire mesh sieve; discard liquid.

2. Combine bulgur, teriyaki sauce, lemon juice and oil in large bowl. Stir in cucumber, tomato, onions, cilantro, ginger and garlic until well blended. Cover; refrigerate 4 hours, stirring occasionally.

Makes 4 servings

Layered Mexican Salad

■ Chili Verde ■

½ to ¾ pound boneless lean pork, cut into 1-inch cubes
1 large onion, halved and thinly sliced
6 cloves garlic, chopped or sliced
1 pound fresh tomatillos
1 can (about 14 ounces) chicken broth
1 can (4 ounces) diced mild green chilies
1 teaspoon ground cumin
1½ cups cooked navy or Great Northern beans *or* 1 can (15 ounces) Great Northern beans, rinsed and drained
½ cup lightly packed fresh cilantro, chopped
Sour cream

1. Place pork, onion, garlic and ½ cup water into large saucepan. Cover; simmer over medium-low heat 30 minutes, stirring occasionally (add more water if necessary). Uncover; boil over medium-high heat until liquid evaporates and meat browns.

2. Stir in tomatillos and broth. Cover; simmer over medium heat 20 minutes or until tomatillos are tender. Tear tomatillos apart with 2 forks. Add chilies and cumin.

3. Cover; simmer over medium-low heat 45 minutes or until meat is tender and tears apart easily. (Add more water or broth to keep liquid level the same.) Add beans; simmer 10 minutes or until heated through. Stir in cilantro. Serve with sour cream. *Makes 4 servings*

■ Gilroy Garlic Soup ■

3 tablespoons olive oil
1 large sweet onion, chopped
1 leek, white part only, washed well and diced
8 cups chicken broth
2 large potatoes, peeled and cubed
15 cloves CHRISTOPHER RANCH Whole Peeled Garlic
1 cup half-and-half
Salt and black pepper
½ cup snipped chives

Heat oil in Dutch oven over medium heat. Add onion and leek; cook and stir until tender. Add broth; bring to a boil. Add potatoes and garlic; simmer for 1 hour. Place potato mixture and half-and-half in food processor; process until smooth. Season to taste with salt and pepper. Top with chives.

Makes 6 to 8 servings

Chili Verde

Chili-Crusted Grilled Chicken Caesar ■ Salad ■

¼ cup lemon juice, divided
4 teaspoons minced garlic, divided
2 teaspoons grated lemon peel
1½ teaspoons dried oregano leaves, divided
1 teaspoon chili powder
1 pound boneless skinless chicken breasts
1 tablespoon olive oil
2 anchovy fillets, minced
1 large head romaine lettuce, cut into 1-inch strips
¼ cup grated Parmesan cheese
Tortilla chips (optional)

1. Combine 1 tablespoon juice, 3 teaspoons garlic, lemon peel, 1 teaspoon oregano and chili powder in small bowl. Rub chicken completely with chili mixture.

2. To prevent sticking, spray grid with nonstick cooking spray. Prepare coals for grilling. Grill chicken 4 to 6 inches above medium-high coals for 5 to 7 minutes or until marks are established and surface is dry. Turn chicken over; grill 3 to 4 minutes or until chicken is no longer pink in center.

3. Combine remaining 3 tablespoons lemon juice, remaining 1 teaspoon garlic, remaining ½ teaspoon oregano, oil and anchovy in large bowl. Add lettuce to bowl; toss to coat with dressing. Sprinkle with cheese; toss.

4. Arrange salad on 4 large plates. Slice chicken. Fan on each salad. Garnish with tortilla chips, if desired. *Makes 4 servings*

Chili-Crusted Grilled Chicken Caesar Salad

VEGETABLES & SIDES

Rosemary-Garlic Mashed Potatoes

2½ pounds Yukon Gold potatoes (5 medium), peeled and cut into 1-inch pieces
1½ teaspoons salt, divided
½ cup heavy cream
½ cup milk
2 tablespoons butter
1 tablespoon minced fresh rosemary *or* 1 teaspoon dried rosemary
1 large head roasted garlic (page 7)
⅛ teaspoon white pepper

Place potato pieces in medium saucepan; add water to cover and 1 teaspoon salt. Bring to a boil over high heat. Reduce heat to medium-low; simmer, uncovered, about 12 to 15 minutes until pieces are tender when pierced with fork. (Do not overcook.) Drain water from pan; cover and set aside.

Place cream, milk, butter and rosemary in small saucepan; heat over medium-high heat about 3 minutes or until butter melts and mixture simmers, stirring often. Mash potatoes with potato masher until smooth. Add roasted garlic and milk mixture; beat with electric mixer until smooth. Beat in remaining ½ teaspoon salt and pepper. Serve hot.

Makes 4 to 6 servings

Rosemary-Garlic Mashed Potatoes

Lemon-Garlic Broccoli over Spaghetti ■ Squash ■

1 spaghetti squash (2 pounds)
1 can (about 14 ounces) chicken broth
10 large cloves garlic, halved
2 tablespoons lemon juice
3 fresh sage leaves
2 cups broccoli florets

1. Place spaghetti squash in large saucepan. Pierce skin with fork. Add enough water to cover. Bring to a boil over high heat. Reduce heat to low; simmer, covered, 20 to 30 minutes or until squash is soft. Cut squash in half lengthwise; remove seeds. Set aside.

2. Meanwhile, combine broth and garlic in small saucepan. Bring to a boil over high heat. Reduce heat to low; simmer 15 minutes or until tender. Remove from heat; cool slightly.

3. Place broth, garlic, juice and sage in food processor; process until smooth. Return mixture to saucepan; keep warm.

4. Combine broccoli and ¼ cup water in large nonstick skillet with tight-fitting lid. Bring to a boil over high heat. Reduce heat to medium. Cover and steam 5 minutes or until broccoli is crisp-tender.

5. Scoop out inside of squash. Place squash and broccoli in medium bowl; pour lemon-garlic mixture over squash mixture. Mix well. Garnish as desired. Serve immediately. *Makes 6 servings*

■ Garlic Stir-Fry ■

¼ cup vegetable oil
4 cloves CHRISTOPHER RANCH Whole Peeled Garlic, crushed
3 small slices fresh ginger
Fresh vegetables cut into bite-size pieces, such as zucchini, broccoli, onions, bell peppers, carrots
½ cup white wine
1 teaspoon salt
½ teaspoon black pepper
Chopped fresh oregano
Chopped fresh parsley
Juice of ½ lemon

Heat oil in large skillet over medium-high heat. Add garlic and ginger; cook and stir until ginger is golden brown. Discard ginger. Add vegetables; stir to coat. Add wine; cook and stir 3 minutes. Add salt, pepper, oregano, parsley and lemon juice to taste. Cook 1 minute more. *Makes 4 to 6 servings*

Lemon-Garlic Broccoli over Spaghetti Squash

Sautéed Garlic ■ Potatoes ■

2 pounds boiling potatoes, peeled and cut into 1-inch pieces
3 tablespoons FILIPPO BERIO® Olive Oil
6 cloves garlic, skins on
1 tablespoon lemon juice
1 tablespoon snipped fresh chives
1 tablespoon chopped fresh parsley
Salt and freshly ground black pepper

Place potatoes in large colander; rinse under cold running water. Drain well; pat dry. In large nonstick skillet, heat olive oil over medium heat. Add potatoes in a single layer. Cook, stirring and turning frequently, 10 minutes or until golden brown. Add garlic. Cover; reduce heat to low and cook very gently, shaking pan and stirring mixture occasionally, 15 to 20 minutes or until potatoes are tender when pierced with fork. Remove garlic; discard skins. In small bowl, crush garlic; stir in lemon juice. Add to potatoes; mix well. Cook 1 to 2 minutes or until heated through. Transfer to serving dish; sprinkle with chives and parsley. Season to taste with salt and pepper. *Makes 4 servings*

Focaccia with Dried Tomatoes and ■ Fontina ■

1 tablespoon olive oil
1 loaf (1 pound) frozen bread dough, thawed according to package directions
1 jar (8 ounces) SONOMA® Marinated Dried Tomatoes, drained, 2 tablespoons oil reserved
4 cloves garlic, minced
⅔ cup sliced black olives
1 tablespoon dried basil
1 teaspoon dried oregano
1 teaspoon dried rosemary
2 cups grated fontina cheese

Preheat oven to 425°F. Oil a 13×9×2-inch baking pan. Roll and stretch dough on lightly floured surface; fit dough into pan.

Combine reserved tomato oil with garlic; brush over dough. Sprinkle olives, basil, oregano and rosemary evenly over dough. Arrange tomatoes on top; cover with cheese.

Bake for 35 to 40 minutes until bread is springy to the touch and golden brown around the edges. (Cover loosely with foil during the last 10 minutes if becoming too brown.) Cut into squares while still warm. *Makes 16 squares*

Sautéed Garlic Potatoes

Grilled Balsamic-Herb ■ Ratatouille ■

2 tablespoons balsamic vinegar
1 tablespoon olive oil
Balsamic-Herb Vinaigrette (recipe follows)
2 yellow or red bell peppers, seeded and halved
1 medium eggplant (about 1 pound)
1 small onion, peeled and quartered
12 mushrooms
2 small yellow zucchini, halved lengthwise
½ pint cherry tomatoes
⅓ cup slivered fresh basil

1. Prepare coals for grilling. Spray medium casserole with nonstick cooking spray; set aside. To make basting mixture, combine vinegar and oil in small bowl; set aside. Prepare Balsamic-Herb Vinaigrette.

2. Grill bell pepper halves, skin side down, on covered grill over hot coals 15 to 25 minutes or until skin is charred. Place in plastic bag 10 minutes. Remove skin and discard. Dice bell peppers; place in casserole and keep warm.

3. Slice eggplant into ½-inch-thick rounds. Thread onion quarters onto metal skewers. Baste eggplant and onion; grill on covered grill over medium coals 20 to 30 minutes or until tender, basting and turning every 10 minutes. Cut eggplant into ½-inch strips. Add onion and eggplant to casserole.

4. Thread mushrooms onto metal skewers. Baste mushrooms and cut sides of zucchini. Grill mushrooms and zucchini on covered grill over medium coals 10 to 15 minutes or until tender, basting and turning once. Cut zucchini into ½-inch slices. Add mushrooms and zucchini to casserole. Thread tomatoes onto skewers. Grill on covered grill over medium coals 5 minutes or until blistered, basting and turning once. Add to casserole. Stir in Balsamic-Herb Vinaigrette and basil. *Makes 6 servings*

Balsamic-Herb Vinaigrette

4 cloves garlic, minced
3 tablespoons balsamic vinegar
1 tablespoon minced fresh oregano
1 tablespoon minced fresh thyme
1 teaspoon Dijon mustard
½ teaspoon black pepper

1. Whisk together all ingredients in small bowl; set aside.

Makes about ¼ cup

Grilled Balsamic-Herb Ratatouille

■ Parmesan Polenta ■

4 cups chicken broth
1¼ cups yellow cornmeal
1 small onion, minced
4 cloves garlic, minced
1 tablespoon minced fresh rosemary *or* 1 teaspoon dried rosemary
½ teaspoon salt
6 tablespoons grated Parmesan cheese
1 tablespoon olive oil, divided

1. Spray 11×7-inch baking pan with nonstick cooking spray; set aside. Spray one side of 7-inch-long sheet of waxed paper with cooking spray; set aside. Combine chicken broth, cornmeal, onion, garlic, rosemary and salt in medium saucepan. Cover and bring to a boil over high heat. Reduce heat to medium and simmer 10 to 15 minutes or until mixture has consistency of thick mashed potatoes. Remove from heat and stir in cheese.

2. Spread polenta evenly in prepared pan; place waxed paper, sprayed side down, on polenta and smooth. (If surface is bumpy, it is more likely to stick to grill.) Cool on wire rack 15 minutes or until firm. Remove waxed paper; cut into 6 squares. Remove squares from pan.

3. To prevent sticking, spray grid with cooking spray. Prepare coals for grilling. Brush tops of squares with half the oil. Grill, oil side down, on covered grill over medium to low coals for 6 to 8 minutes or until golden. Brush with remaining oil and gently turn over. Grill 6 to 8 minutes more or until golden. Serve warm.

Makes 6 servings

■ Lemon Garlic Greens ■

1½ pounds beet greens
2 teaspoons olive oil
¼ cup finely chopped onion
4 cloves garlic, minced
2 tablespoons lemon juice
¼ teaspoon salt
¼ teaspoon black pepper

Wash beet greens. Drain but do not pat dry; leave some water clinging to leaves. Remove stems; coarsely chop.

Heat oil in large saucepan over medium heat. Add beet greens, onion and garlic; cook and stir 5 minutes. Stir in lemon juice, salt and pepper; continue cooking about 5 minutes or until greens are wilted and onion is tender. Serve warm. *Makes 4 servings*

Parmesan Polenta

Orzo with Spinach ■ and Red Pepper ■

- 4 ounces uncooked orzo (rice-shaped pasta)
- 1 tablespoon olive oil
- 1 red bell pepper, stemmed, seeded and diced
- 4 cloves garlic, minced
- 1 package (10 ounces) frozen chopped spinach, thawed and squeezed dry
- ¼ cup grated Parmesan cheese
- ½ teaspoon minced fresh oregano or basil (optional)
- ¼ teaspoon lemon pepper

1. Prepare orzo according to package directions; drain well. Set aside.

2. Heat oil in large skillet over medium-high heat. Add bell pepper and garlic; cook and stir 2 to 3 minutes or until bell pepper is crisp-tender. Add orzo and spinach; stir until evenly mixed and heated through. Remove from heat and stir in Parmesan cheese, oregano, if desired, and lemon pepper. Garnish as desired.

Makes 6 servings

Orzo with Spinach and Red Pepper

Stuffed Jumbo Shells with ■ Garlic Vegetables ■

Garlic Vegetables (recipe follows)
2 cups ricotta cheese
1 package (10 ounces) frozen chopped spinach, thawed and squeezed dry
¼ cup grated Parmesan cheese
2 cloves garlic, minced
¾ teaspoon dried marjoram leaves
½ to 1 teaspoon salt
½ teaspoon dried basil leaves
½ teaspoon black pepper
¼ teaspoon dried thyme leaves
12 jumbo pasta shells, cooked according to package directions, drained and cooled
Grated Parmesan cheese

Prepare Garlic Vegetables. Spoon into 10-inch round baking dish.

Combine ricotta, spinach, ¼ cup grated Parmesan cheese, garlic, marjoram, salt, basil, pepper and thyme in medium bowl. Spoon cheese mixture into shells.

Preheat oven to 350°F. Arrange shells on top of Garlic Vegetables. Carefully spoon sauce from vegetables over shells. Bake, loosely covered with foil, 35 to 40 minutes or until stuffed shells are heated through. Sprinkle Parmesan cheese over shells. *Makes 4 servings*

Garlic Vegetables

2 tablespoons olive oil, divided
1 large head garlic, coarsely chopped
⅓ cup sun-dried tomatoes (not packed in oil)
2 tablespoons all-purpose flour
1¼ cups canned vegetable broth
2 large carrots, sliced diagonally
1 medium zucchini, halved and sliced
1 medium yellow summer squash, halved and sliced
2 tablespoons minced fresh parsley
Salt and black pepper

Stuffed Jumbo Shells with Garlic Vegetables

Heat 1 tablespoon oil in small skillet over medium heat. Add garlic; cook and stir 2 to 3 minutes. Reduce heat to low and cook about 15 minutes or until garlic is golden brown, stirring frequently. Add tomatoes; cook over medium heat 2 minutes. Stir in flour. Cook and stir 2 minutes. Gradually stir in vegetable broth. Cook 1 to 2 minutes or until sauce thickens, stirring constantly.

Heat remaining 1 tablespoon oil in medium skillet over medium heat. Add carrots; cook and stir 2 minutes. Add zucchini and squash; cook and stir 3 minutes or until crisp-tender. Remove from heat. Stir garlic mixture and parsley into carrot mixture in skillet. Season to taste with salt and pepper. *Makes 2 cups*

Garlic Shrimp with ■ Noodles ■

4 tablespoons butter, divided
¼ cup finely chopped onion
2 cups water
1 package LIPTON® Noodles & Sauce—Butter & Herb
2 tablespoons olive oil
1 tablespoon finely chopped garlic
1 pound medium shrimp, shelled and deveined
1 can (14 ounces) artichoke hearts, drained and halved
¼ cup finely chopped fresh parsley
Black pepper to taste

In 2-quart microwave-safe casserole, microwave 2 tablespoons butter and onion, uncovered, at HIGH 2 minutes or until tender. Stir in water and Noodles & Butter & Herb Sauce; microwave 11 minutes or until noodles are tender. Stir; cover and set aside.

In 1-quart microwave-safe casserole or 9-inch glass pie plate, microwave remaining 2 tablespoons butter, olive oil and garlic, uncovered, at HIGH 2 minutes. Stir in shrimp and artichokes. Microwave at HIGH 3 minutes or until shrimp are opaque, stirring once. Stir in parsley and pepper to taste.

Combine shrimp mixture with noodles; microwave, covered, at HIGH 1 minute or until heated through. Let stand, covered, 2 minutes.

Makes about 4 servings

Pasta Twists with ■ Spinach Pesto ■

1 bunch spinach, washed, stemmed and torn
1 cup fresh parsley sprigs
⅔ cup grated Parmesan cheese
½ cup walnut pieces
6 cloves garlic, crushed
2 anchovy filets
1 teaspoon dried basil leaves
1 teaspoon salt
1 teaspoon black pepper
1 cup olive oil
Pasta twists, cooked according to package directions, drained

Place spinach, parsley, cheese, walnuts, garlic, anchovies, basil, salt and pepper in food processor. Process until smooth.

With processor running, add oil in thin stream. Adjust seasonings, if desired. Pour desired amount of pesto over pasta; toss gently to coat.

Makes 4 servings

Pasta Twists with Spinach Pesto

Spinach Fettuccine with Garlic-Onion ■ Sauce ■

- ½ cup butter
- 1 tablespoon olive oil
- 1 pound Vidalia or other sweet onions, sliced
- 12 cloves garlic, chopped
- 1 tablespoon honey
- ¼ cup Marsala wine
- Salt and black pepper
- 1 pound spinach fettuccine, cooked according to package directions, drained
- Grated Parmesan cheese (optional)

Heat butter and oil in large skillet over medium heat. Add onions and garlic; cover and cook until soft. Add honey; reduce heat to low. Cook, uncovered, 30 minutes, stirring occasionally. Add wine; cook 5 to 10 minutes more. Season to taste with salt and pepper. Toss sauce over pasta; sprinkle with Parmesan cheese and serve.

Makes 4 servings

Pasta with Zucchini ■ and Roasted Garlic ■

- 8 medium cloves garlic, peeled
- ½ teaspoon dried thyme leaves
- ½ teaspoon dried rosemary
- 2 tablespoons vegetable oil
- 1 pound rotini, twists or spirals, uncooked
- 3 medium zucchini, coarsely grated (about 5 to 6 cups)
- Salt and black pepper

Preheat oven to 450°F. Lay 12-inch square piece of foil on counter; place garlic cloves on top. Sprinkle thyme and rosemary over the garlic. Pour oil over garlic and herbs. Draw up edges of foil and make a sealed packet. Bake 20 minutes.

Meanwhile, cook pasta according to package directions. Two minutes before pasta is done, add zucchini to pasta. Cook two minutes. Drain zucchini and pasta.

Open foil packet and mash garlic lightly with spoon. Toss with pasta and zucchini; season to taste with salt and pepper and serve.

Makes 4 servings

Favorite recipe from **National Pasta Association**

Spinach Fettuccine with Garlic-Onion Sauce

Summer Garden ■ Harvest Fusilli ■

- ¼ cup olive oil
- 8 ounces mushrooms, trimmed and sliced
- 1 red bell pepper, diced
- 1 green bell pepper, diced
- 1 yellow bell pepper, diced
- 3 shallots, chopped
- 10 green onions, chopped
- 1 large onion, chopped
- 8 cloves garlic, crushed
- ¼ teaspoon red pepper flakes
- 4 cups chopped seeded tomatoes
- ½ cup chopped fresh basil
- 2 tablespoons chopped fresh oregano
- Salt and black pepper
- 1 package (16 ounces) fusilli, cooked according to package directions, drained

Heat oil in large skillet over medium-high heat. Cook and stir mushrooms, bell peppers, shallots, onions, garlic and red pepper flakes until lightly browned. Add tomatoes with juice; bring to a boil. Reduce heat to low; simmer, uncovered, 20 minutes. Stir in basil and oregano. Season to taste with salt and black pepper.

Place fusilli on plates. Spoon sauce over fusilli. Garnish, if desired.

Makes 6 to 8 servings

Thailand Peanut ■ Pesto ■

- 1 cup unsalted roasted peanuts
- ½ cup soy sauce
- ½ cup sesame oil
- 1 teaspoon TABASCO® pepper sauce
- ¼ cup honey
- ⅓ cup water
- 3 cloves garlic, minced
- 12 ounces bow tie pasta, cooked according to package directions, drained
- Chopped scallions for garnish

Place peanuts in food processor; process until finely ground. With motor running, add soy sauce, sesame oil, TABASCO® sauce, honey, water and garlic, one at a time, through the feed tube. Process until a thick, smooth paste has formed. Transfer the mixture to a bowl; refrigerate, covered, until ready to use. Toss with bow tie pasta and garnish with chopped scallions.

Makes 4 servings

Summer Garden Harvest Fusilli

■ Hearty Cassoulet ■

- 1 tablespoon olive oil
- 1 large onion, finely chopped
- 4 boneless skinless chicken thighs (about 1 pound), diced
- ¼ pound smoked turkey sausage, finely chopped
- 3 cloves garlic, minced
- 3 cans (about 15 ounces each) Great Northern beans, rinsed and drained
- 4 tablespoons tomato paste
- 1 teaspoon dried thyme leaves
- ½ teaspoon black pepper
- ½ cup bread crumbs
- 3 tablespoons minced fresh parsley

1. Heat oil in ovenproof Dutch oven over medium-high heat. Add onion; cook and stir 5 minutes or until onion is tender. Stir in chicken, sausage and garlic; cook 5 minutes or until chicken and sausage are browned, stirring occasionally.

2. Stir beans, ¼ cup water, tomato paste, thyme and pepper into Dutch oven. Cover; reduce heat to medium-low. Simmer 15 minutes or until mixture is bubbly.

3. Preheat broiler. Combine bread crumbs and parsley in small bowl; sprinkle over top of cassoulet. Broil, 4 inches from heat, 3 minutes or until bread crumbs are lightly browned. *Makes 6 servings*

Hearty Cassoulet

Spicy Island ■ Chicken ■

- 1 onion, finely chopped
- ⅓ cup white wine vinegar
- 6 green onions, finely chopped
- 6 cloves garlic, minced
- 1 habañero or serrano pepper,* finely chopped
- 2 tablespoons olive oil
- 4½ teaspoons fresh thyme leaves *or* 2 teaspoons dried thyme leaves
- 1 tablespoon ground allspice
- 2 teaspoons sugar
- 1 teaspoon salt
- 1 teaspoon ground cinnamon
- 1 teaspoon ground nutmeg
- 1 teaspoon black pepper
- ½ teaspoon ground red pepper
- 6 boneless skinless chicken breast halves

**Chili peppers can sting and irritate the skin; wear rubber gloves when handling peppers and do not touch eyes. Wash hands after handling.*

1. To prepare marinade, combine onion, vinegar, green onions, garlic, habañero pepper, olive oil, thyme, allspice, sugar, salt, cinnamon, nutmeg, black pepper and red pepper; mix well. Place chicken and marinade in resealable plastic food storage bag; turn bag to coat. Marinate in refrigerator 4 hours or overnight.

2. To prevent sticking, spray grid with nonstick cooking spray. Prepare coals for grilling. Drain chicken; reserve marinade. Place chicken on grill, 4 to 6 inches from medium-high coals. Grill 5 to 7 minutes on each side or until no longer pink in center, brushing occasionally with marinade. Discard remaining marinade. Serve with grilled sweet potatoes, if desired. *Makes 6 servings*

Spicy Island Chicken

Jamaican Rum ■ Chicken ■

- ½ cup dark rum
- 2 tablespoons lime juice or lemon juice
- 2 tablespoons soy sauce
- 2 tablespoons brown sugar
- 4 large cloves garlic, minced
- 1 to 2 jalapeño peppers,* seeded and minced
- 1 tablespoon minced fresh ginger
- 1 teaspoon dried thyme leaves
- ½ teaspoon black pepper
- 6 boneless skinless chicken breast halves

**Jalapeño peppers can sting and irritate the skin; wear rubber gloves when handling peppers and do not touch eyes. Wash hands after handling.*

To prepare marinade, combine rum, lime juice, soy sauce, sugar, garlic, jalapeños, ginger, thyme and pepper in small bowl. Place chicken in resealable plastic food storage bag. Pour marinade over chicken. Press air out of bag and seal tightly. Turn bag over to completely coat chicken with marinade. Refrigerate 4 hours or overnight, turning bag once or twice.

To prevent sticking, spray grill with nonstick cooking spray. Prepare coals for grilling. Drain chicken; reserve marinade. Grill chicken, 3 to 4 inches from medium-high coals, 5 to 7 minutes on each side or until no longer pink in center.

Meanwhile, bring reserved marinade to a boil in small saucepan over medium-high heat. Boil 5 minutes or until marinade is reduced by about half. To serve, drizzle marinade over chicken. Garnish as desired.

Makes 6 servings

Jamaican Rum Chicken

French Pan-Roasted ■ Hens ■

- 1 package (about 3 pounds) PERDUE® Fresh Split Cornish Hens
- 3 tablespoons olive oil, divided
- 1 tablespoon herbes de Provence
- Salt and black pepper
- 3 garlic cloves, peeled, divided
- ½ cup white wine or water

Rub hens with 1 tablespoon oil; sprinkle with herbes de Provence, and salt and pepper to taste. Heat remaining 2 tablespoons oil in large, deep skillet over medium-high heat. Add hens and 2 garlic cloves. Brown hens lightly on both sides. Discard cooked garlic and add remaining garlic clove. Reduce heat to low; cover and cook 30 to 40 minutes until hens are browned and cooked through, turning 2 to 3 times.

Remove to warm serving platter; discard garlic. Add wine to skillet; cook 1 minute, stirring to incorporate pan juices. Serve hens with pan sauce.

Makes 2 to 4 servings

■ Turkey Jambalaya ■

- 1 tablespoon vegetable oil, divided
- 6 ounces turkey ham, cut into ½-inch cubes
- 6 ounces fully cooked smoked turkey sausage or kielbasa, cut into ¼-inch slices
- 1½ cups chopped onions
- 1½ cups ¼-inch celery slices
- 1 cup ½-inch green bell pepper cubes
- 4 to 5 cloves garlic, minced
- 2 tablespoons Creole seasoning
- 1¼ cups uncooked long-grain rice
- 2 cups turkey or chicken broth
- 1 can (15 ounces) tomato sauce

1. Heat 1 teaspoon oil in large saucepan over medium heat. Add turkey ham and sausage; cook and stir until lightly browned on all sides. Remove from pan; set aside.

2. Heat remaining oil in same saucepan. Add onions, celery, bell pepper, garlic and Creole seasoning; cook and stir about 10 minutes or until vegetables are crisp-tender.

3. Add rice; cook an additional 5 minutes, stirring constantly to prevent sticking. Add turkey broth, tomato sauce and reserved turkey ham and sausage; bring to a boil. Reduce heat; cover and simmer 25 to 30 minutes or until rice is tender. *Makes 4 servings*

Favorite recipe from **National Turkey Federation**

Roasted Chicken and Veggies

1 chicken (3 to 5 pounds), washed and patted dry
6 CHRISTOPHER RANCH Pearl Onions, peeled
6 cloves CHRISTOPHER RANCH Elephant Garlic, peeled
6 CHRISTOPHER RANCH Shallots, peeled
6 small carrots, peeled and cut in half crosswise
3 potatoes, scrubbed and cut in ½-inch slices
¼ cup olive oil
½ cup white wine
Italian seasoning
Seasoned salt
Lemon pepper
4 fresh rosemary sprigs

Place chicken in large baking dish. Toss onions, garlic, shallots, carrots and potatoes with olive oil in large bowl to coat; place around chicken. Pour wine over vegetables and chicken; season to taste with Italian seasoning, seasoned salt and lemon pepper. Place rosemary sprigs over chicken and vegetables. Bake at 450°F for 1 to 1½ hours, basting frequently. Remove rosemary sprigs before serving. *Makes 4 servings*

Note: Onions, garlic and shallots have a milder flavor when baked, so serve them along with the other baked vegetables.

Turkey & Zucchini Enchiladas with Tomatillo-Green ■ Chili Sauce ■

1¼ pounds turkey leg
Tomatillo-Green Chili Sauce (page 57)
1 tablespoon olive oil
1 small onion, thinly sliced
1 tablespoon minced garlic (5 to 6 cloves)
1 pound zucchini, quartered lengthwise, sliced thinly crosswise
1½ teaspoons ground cumin
½ teaspoon dried oregano leaves
¾ cup (3 ounces) shredded Monterey Jack cheese
12 (6-inch) corn tortillas
½ cup crumbled feta cheese
6 sprigs fresh cilantro for garnish

1. Place turkey in large saucepan; cover with water. Bring to a boil over high heat. Reduce heat to medium-low. Cover and simmer 1½ to 2 hours or until meat pulls apart easily when tested with fork. Drain; discard skin and bone. Cut meat into small pieces. Place in medium bowl; set aside.

2. Prepare Tomatillo-Green Chili Sauce.

3. Heat oil in large skillet over medium-high heat. Add onion; cook and stir 3 to 4 minutes or until tender. Reduce heat to medium. Add garlic; cook and stir 3 to 4 minutes or until onion is golden. Add zucchini, 2 tablespoons water, cumin and oregano. Cover; cook and stir over medium heat 10 minutes or until zucchini is tender. Add to turkey. Stir in Monterey Jack cheese.

4. Preheat oven to 350°F. Heat large nonstick skillet over medium-high heat. Place 1 inch water in medium bowl. Dip 1 tortilla in water; shake off excess. Place in hot skillet. Cook 10 to 15 seconds on each side or until tortilla is hot and pliable. Repeat with remaining tortillas.

5. Spray bottom of 13×9-inch baking pan with nonstick cooking spray. Spoon ¼ cup filling in center of each tortilla; fold sides over to enclose. Place, seam side down, in pan. Brush tops with ½ cup Tomatillo-Green Chili Sauce. Cover and bake 30 to 40 minutes or until heated through. Top enchiladas with remaining Tomatillo-Green Chili Sauce and feta cheese. Garnish with cilantro.

Makes 6 servings

Tomatillo-Green Chili Sauce

- ¾ pound fresh tomatillos *or* 2 cans (18 ounces each) whole tomatillos, drained
- 1 can (4 ounces) diced mild green chilies, drained
- ½ cup chicken broth
- 1 teaspoon dried oregano leaves
- ½ teaspoon ground cumin
- 2 tablespoons chopped fresh cilantro (optional)

1. Place tomatillos in large saucepan; cover with water. Bring to a boil over high heat. Reduce heat to medium-high and simmer gently 20 to 30 minutes or until tomatillos are tender. Drain.

2. Place tomatillos, chilies, chicken broth (omit if using canned tomatillos), oregano and cumin in food processor or blender; process until smooth. Return mixture to pan. Cover; heat over medium heat until bubbling. Stir in cilantro, if desired. *Makes about 3 cups*

Turkey & Zucchini Enchiladas with Tomatillo-Green Chili Sauce

Turkey Breast Braised with Garlic and Rice

- 1 cup uncooked long-grain rice
- 1 can (about 14 ounces) chicken broth
- ½ cup white wine
- 2 teaspoons dried parsley flakes
- ½ teaspoon dried rosemary
- ½ teaspoon dried thyme leaves
- ½ teaspoon dried sage leaves
- 1 bay leaf
- 1 bone-in turkey breast (6 pounds)
- Paprika
- 3 heads of garlic, root-end cut off

1. Combine rice, chicken broth, wine, parsley, rosemary, thyme, sage and bay leaf in ovenproof Dutch oven. Place turkey over rice mixture and sprinkle turkey generously with paprika. Place whole garlic heads, cut end up, in rice around turkey breast. Cover top of ovenproof Dutch oven with foil and lid. Bake at 350°F 2½ to 3 hours or until meat thermometer inserted in thickest part of breast registers 170° to 175°F. Allow to stand 10 to 15 minutes. Remove bay leaf; discard.

Turkey Breast Braised with Garlic and Rice

2. To serve, carve turkey into slices and place on platter. Spoon rice mixture into serving bowl. Squeeze garlic from skins onto turkey and rice. *Makes 4 servings*

Favorite recipe from **National Turkey Federation**

■ Ginger Hot Thighs ■

2 tablespoons olive oil
1 package (about 1¾ pounds) PERDUE® Fresh Skinless Chicken Thighs
1 onion, finely chopped
¼ cup red wine
4 garlic cloves, minced
1 tablespoon grated fresh ginger
1½ teaspoons ground cumin
½ teaspoon chili powder
1 tablespoon minced fresh parsley

Heat oil in large nonstick skillet over medium heat. Add chicken; cook 7 to 8 minutes on each side or until browned. Combine onion, wine, garlic, ginger, cumin and chili powder in small bowl. Add to skillet; partially cover and reduce heat to medium-low. Cook about 20 to 30 minutes or until chicken is fork-tender and liquid has been reduced to a glaze. Sprinkle with parsley and serve.

Makes 3 to 4 servings

■ Forty Clove Chicken ■

3 pounds chicken pieces
40 cloves CHRISTOPHER RANCH Whole Peeled Garlic (unpeeled cloves may also be used)
½ cup dry white wine
¼ cup dry vermouth
¼ cup olive oil
4 ribs celery, cut into 1-inch pieces
2 teaspoons dry basil leaves, crushed
1 teaspoon dry oregano leaves, crushed
6 sprigs fresh parsley, minced
Pinch of red pepper flakes
Salt and black pepper
1 lemon, cut in half

Preheat oven to 375°F. Place chicken in shallow baking pan, skin side up. Sprinkle chicken evenly with garlic, wine, vermouth, oil, celery, basil, oregano, parsley, red pepper, and salt and black pepper to taste. Squeeze juice from lemon over top. Cut lemon peel into pieces and arrange throughout chicken. Cover with foil and bake for 40 minutes. Remove foil and bake an additional 15 minutes. Serve garlic cloves with chicken or spread on sliced French bread. (If left unpeeled, just squeeze out pulp.) *Makes 4 servings*

Baked Chicken with Crispy Cheese-Garlic ■ Crust ■

- 1 teaspoon olive oil
- ½ cup chopped garlic (one large head)
- 4 tablespoons water, divided
- ½ cup dry bread crumbs
- ¼ cup Dijon mustard (or more to taste)
- 1 cup (4 ounces) shredded JARLSBERG Cheese
- 3 pounds chicken pieces, skin removed and trimmed of fat

Preheat oven to 400°F. Heat oil in large skillet over high heat. Add garlic; cook and stir 2 minutes. Add 2 tablespoons water; cover tightly. Reduce heat to low; cook 4 minutes.

Meanwhile, mix crumbs and mustard. Add garlic and blend well. Add cheese plus remaining 2 tablespoons water and mix to make a paste.

Arrange chicken on rack in foil-lined baking pan. Pat thin layer of garlic-cheese paste on top side of chicken pieces to form a crust. Bake, loosely tented with foil, 1 hour or until juices run clear when pierced with a knife.

Makes 3 to 4 servings

Garlic Chicken and ■ Corn Stir-Fry ■

- 4 boneless skinless chicken thighs, cut into 1-inch squares
- 1 tablespoon soy sauce
- 4 cloves garlic, minced
- ¼ teaspoon black pepper
- ½ cup chicken broth
- ¾ teaspoon onion powder
- 1½ teaspoons cornstarch
- 2 teaspoons vegetable oil
- 1 large red bell pepper, cut into 1-inch squares
- 2 large ribs celery, cut into 1-inch slices
- 1 package (10 ounces) frozen corn, thawed and drained
- 2 cups hot cooked rice

Place chicken in small bowl. Add soy sauce, garlic and black pepper; stir to coat. Marinate 15 minutes at room temperature.

Meanwhile, stir chicken broth and onion powder into cornstarch in small bowl until smooth; set aside. Heat oil in wok over high heat. Reduce heat to medium-high. Add chicken; stir-fry 2 minutes. Add bell pepper and celery; stir-fry 2 minutes. Add corn; cook and stir 3 minutes. Stir in cornstarch mixture; cook and stir over high heat until mixture boils and slightly thickens. Serve over rice.

Makes 4 servings

Jen's Ginger-Garlic ■ Chicken Drummettes ■

½ cup soy sauce
¼ cup white wine
2 teaspoons sugar
2 teaspoons CHRISTOPHER RANCH Chopped Ginger *or* 1 teaspoon fresh grated ginger
Juice of 2 to 3 lemons
3 cloves CHRISTOPHER RANCH Whole Peeled Garlic, crushed
14 chicken drummettes

To prepare marinade, combine soy sauce, wine, sugar, ginger, lemon juice and garlic in small bowl. Place drummettes in resealable plastic food storage bag. Pour marinade over drummettes. Press air out of bag and seal tightly. Turn bag over to completely coat drummettes with marinade. Refrigerate 6 hours or overnight, turning bag once or twice. Place drummettes with marinade in a large glass baking dish sprayed with nonstick cooking spray. Bake at 350°F for 1 hour or until juices run clear. Marinade should form a glaze on drummettes. *Makes 4 servings*

Garlicky Chicken ■ Packets ■

1 cup julienned carrots
½ cup sliced onion
¼ cup chopped fresh basil *or* 1 tablespoon dried basil leaves, crushed
2 tablespoons mayonnaise
6 cloves garlic, minced
⅛ teaspoon black pepper
4 boneless skinless chicken breast halves

Cut parchment paper or foil into four 12-inch squares. Fold squares in half, then cut into shape of half hearts. Open parchment to form whole hearts.

Preheat oven to 400°F. Place carrots and onion on 1 side of each heart near fold. Combine basil, mayonnaise, garlic and pepper in small bowl; spread mixture on chicken. Place chicken, mayonnaise side up, on top of vegetables. Fold parchment over chicken; seal by creasing and folding edges of parchment in small overlapping sections from top of heart until completed at point. Finish by twisting point and tucking under.

Place parchment packages on ungreased baking sheet. Bake 20 to 25 minutes or until juices run clear and chicken is no longer pink in center. *Makes 4 servings*

SEAFOOD

Baked Shrimp with Chili-Garlic Butter

- ½ cup butter
- ¼ cup vegetable oil
- 8 cloves garlic, finely chopped
- 1 to 3 dried de arbol chilies, coarsely crumbled*
- 1 tablespoon lime juice
- ¼ teaspoon salt
- 1½ pounds medium shrimp, peeled and deveined, tails attached
- Green onion tops, slivered, for garnish

**Note: For milder flavor, seed some or all of the chilies.*

Preheat oven to 400°F. Heat butter and oil in small skillet over medium heat until butter is melted and foamy. Add garlic, chilies, lime juice and salt; cook and stir 1 minute. Remove from heat.

Arrange shrimp in even layer in shallow 2-quart gratin pan or baking dish. Pour hot butter mixture over shrimp. Bake 10 to 12 minutes until shrimp turn pink and opaque, stirring once. *Do not overcook or shrimp will be dry and tough.* Garnish with green onion tops. *Makes 4 servings*

Baked Shrimp with Chili-Garlic Butter

Baked Rockfish ■ Veracruz ■

1 teaspoon olive oil
½ small onion, chopped
4 cloves garlic, minced
8 to 10 ounces tomatoes, cored and chopped *or* 2 cans (15 ounces each) whole tomatoes, drained and chopped
½ green bell pepper, chopped
½ to 1 jalapeño pepper,* seeded and minced
1 teaspoon dried oregano leaves
½ teaspoon ground cumin
¼ cup small pimiento-stuffed green olives
2 teaspoons drained capers
1 pound skinless rockfish, snapper or cod fillets
2 cups hot cooked rice

**Jalapeño peppers can sting and irritate the skin; wear rubber gloves when handling peppers and do not touch eyes. Wash hands after handling.*

1. Preheat oven to 375°F. Heat oil in large nonstick skillet over medium-high heat. Add onion and garlic; cook and stir 3 minutes or until onion is tender. Add tomatoes, bell pepper, jalapeño, oregano and cumin; cook over high heat, stirring occasionally, 2 to 3 minutes more. Stir in olives and capers; set aside.

2. Spray 11×7-inch baking pan with nonstick cooking spray. Place fish in single layer in pan, folding thin tail sections under to make fish evenly thick. Pour tomato mixture over fish. Cover with foil; bake 10 minutes or until fish is opaque and flakes easily when tested with fork. Serve with rice and garnish with fresh herbs, if desired.

Makes 4 servings

Lemon-Garlic ■ Grilling Sauce ■

½ cup butter or margarine, melted
¼ cup lemon juice
1 tablespoon Worcestershire sauce
3 cloves garlic, peeled and minced
½ teaspoon TABASCO® pepper sauce
¼ teaspoon black pepper

Combine butter, lemon juice, Worcestershire sauce, garlic, TABASCO® sauce and black pepper in small bowl; mix well. Brush on fish, seafood, poultry or vegetables during grilling or broiling. Heat any remaining sauce and serve with grilled foods. *Makes ¾ cup*

Baked Rockfish Veracruz

Crab and Corn Enchilada Casserole

- Spicy Tomato Sauce (page 67), divided
- 10 to 12 ounces fresh crabmeat
- 1 package (10 ounces) frozen corn, thawed and drained
- 1½ cups (6 ounces) shredded Monterey Jack cheese, divided
- 1 can (4 ounces) diced mild green chilies
- 12 (6-inch) corn tortillas
- 1 lime, cut into 6 wedges
- Sour cream

1. Preheat oven to 350°F. Prepare Spicy Tomato Sauce.

2. Combine 2 cups Spicy Tomato Sauce, crabmeat, corn, 1 cup cheese and chilies in medium bowl.

3. Cut each tortilla into 4 wedges. Place one third of tortilla wedges on bottom of shallow 3- to 4-quart casserole, overlapping to make solid layer. Spread half of crabmeat mixture on top. Repeat with another layer tortilla wedges, remaining crabmeat mixture and remaining tortillas. Spread remaining 1 cup Spicy Tomato Sauce over top; cover.

Crab and Corn Enchilada Casserole

4. Bake 30 to 40 minutes or until heated through. Sprinkle with remaining ½ cup cheese and bake, uncovered, 5 minutes or until cheese melts. Serve with lime wedges and sour cream.

Makes 6 servings

Spicy Tomato Sauce

2 cans (15 ounces each) stewed tomatoes, undrained
2 teaspoons olive oil
1 medium onion, chopped
1 tablespoon minced garlic
2 tablespoons chili powder
2 teaspoons ground cumin
2 teaspoons dried oregano
1 teaspoon ground cinnamon
¼ teaspoon red pepper flakes
¼ teaspoon ground cloves

1. Combine tomatoes with liquid in food processor; process until finely chopped. Set aside.

2. Heat oil over medium-high heat in large saucepan or Dutch oven. Add onion and garlic. Cook and stir 5 minutes or until onion is tender. Add chili powder, cumin, oregano, cinnamon, red pepper and cloves. Cook and stir 1 minute.

3. Add tomatoes; reduce heat to medium-low. Simmer, uncovered, 20 minutes or until sauce is reduced to 3 cups.

Makes about 3 cups

■ Shrimp Scampi ■

⅓ cup clarified butter*
4 tablespoons minced garlic
1½ pounds large shrimp, peeled and deveined
6 green onions, thinly sliced
¼ cup dry white wine
2 tablespoons lemon juice
8 large sprigs fresh parsley, finely chopped
Salt
Black pepper
Lemon slices and fresh parsley sprigs, for garnish

**To clarify butter, melt butter over low heat. Skim off the white foam that forms on top, then strain clear golden butter through cheesecloth into container. Discard milky residue at the bottom of pan. Clarified butter will keep, covered, in refrigerator for up to 2 months.*

Heat clarified butter in large skillet over medium heat. Add garlic; cook and stir 1 to 2 minutes or until soft but not brown. Add shrimp, onions, wine and lemon juice; cook until shrimp turn pink and firm, 1 to 2 minutes on each side. *Do not overcook.* Add chopped parsley; season to taste with salt and pepper. Garnish with lemon slices and fresh parsley sprigs. Serve immediately. *Makes 4 servings*

■ Garlic Clams ■

- **2 pounds littleneck clams**
- **Salt**
- **2 teaspoons olive oil**
- **2 tablespoons finely chopped onion**
- **2 tablespoons chopped garlic**
- **½ cup dry white wine**
- **¼ cup chopped red bell pepper**
- **2 tablespoons lemon juice**
- **1 tablespoon chopped fresh parsley**

1. Discard any clams that remain open when tapped with fingers. To clean clams, scrub with stiff brush under cold running water. Soak clams in mixture of ⅓ cup salt to 1 gallon water 20 minutes. Drain water; repeat 2 more times.

2. Heat oil in large saucepan over medium-high heat. Add onion and garlic; cook and stir about 3 minutes or until garlic is tender but not brown. Add wine, bell pepper, lemon juice and clams. Cover and simmer 3 to 10 minutes or until clams open. Transfer clams as they open to large bowl, covering to keep warm. Discard any clams that do not open. Increase heat to high. Add parsley; boil until liquid is reduced to ¼ to ⅓ cup. Pour over clams; serve immediately.

Makes 4 servings

Fish Fantastic and ■ Fast ■

- **4 fish fillets or steaks* (about 6 ounces each)**
- **¼ cup SONOMA® Dried Tomato Bits**
- **¼ cup lemon juice**
- **2 tablespoons chopped fresh thyme**
- **4 teaspoons minced garlic**
- **Salt and black pepper**

**Note: Choose any thick-fleshed fish such as halibut, sea bass and orange roughy.*

Preheat oven to 400°F. Cut parchment paper or foil into four 12-inch squares. Fold squares in half, then cut into shape of half hearts. Open parchment to form whole hearts.

Place one fish fillet on one side of each heart near fold. Top fish with tomato bits, lemon juice, thyme and garlic, dividing equally. Season to taste with salt and pepper. Fold parchment over fish. Seal by creasing and folding edges of parchment in small overlapping sections from top of heart until completed at point. Twist point and tuck under. Place parchment packages on baking sheet. Bake 10 to 12 minutes until packets are browned and puffed.

Makes 4 servings

Garlic Clams

■ Seafood Paella ■

6 to 7 cups Fish Stock (recipe follows), heated, divided
1 pound small squid, cleaned
16 mussels, cleaned and debearded
Salt
½ cup olive oil
2 green bell peppers, chopped
1 medium onion, chopped
8 cloves garlic, minced
2 cups uncooked rice
1 teaspoon ground turmeric
1 teaspoon paprika
1 bay leaf
1 can (16 ounces) tomatoes, drained and chopped
½ cup dry white wine
1 pound cod, monkfish or other firm white fish, rinsed, patted dry and cut into 1-inch pieces
½ pound medium shrimp, peeled and deveined
½ pound scallops
1 cup fresh or frozen peas
¼ cup chopped fresh parsley
1 jar (2 ounces) sliced pimientos, drained

Prepare Fish Stock. Cut squid body sac crosswise into ¼-inch rings; finely chop tentacles and fins. Pat dry with paper towels. Soak mussels in mixture of ⅓ cup salt to 1 gallon water 20 minutes. Drain water; repeat 2 more times.

Preheat oven to 375°F. Heat oil in 14- to 15-inch paella pan or heavy large skillet over medium-high heat. Add bell peppers, onion and garlic; cook and stir 5 to 8 minutes or until tender. Stir in rice, 2 teaspoons salt, turmeric, paprika and bay leaf. Reduce heat to medium. Add 5 cups Fish Stock, tomatoes and wine. Simmer 15 to 20 minutes, adding additional stock as needed until rice is almost tender, stirring frequently.

Stir in squid, cod, shrimp, scallops, peas and parsley. Garnish top of paella with pimientos and mussels. Place paella in oven and bake 15 minutes or until seafood is opaque and liquid is absorbed. Remove bay leaf; discard. Serve immediately. *Makes 8 servings*

Fish Stock

1¾ pounds fish skeletons and heads from lean fish, such as red snapper, cod, halibut or flounder
2 medium onions, cut into wedges
3 ribs celery, cut into 2-inch pieces
2 slices lemon
¾ teaspoon dried thyme leaves
8 black peppercorns
3 fresh parsley leaves
1 bay leaf
1 clove garlic

Seafood Paella

Rinse fish; cut out gills and discard. Combine fish skeletons and heads, onions and celery in stockpot or Dutch oven. Add 10 cups cold water, lemon, thyme, peppercorns, parsley, bay leaf and garlic. Bring to a boil over high heat. Reduce heat to medium-low; simmer, uncovered, 30 minutes, skimming foam that rises to the surface.

Remove stock from heat and cool slightly. Strain stock through large sieve or colander lined with several layers of dampened cheesecloth, removing all bones and seasonings; discard. Use immediately or refrigerate stock in tightly covered container up to 2 days or freeze stock in freezer containers for several months.

Makes about 10 cups stock

BEEF, LAMB & PORK

Tenderloins with Roasted Garlic Sauce

2 heads roasted garlic (page 7)
⅔ cup A.1. ORIGINAL® or A.1. BOLD® Steak Sauce, divided
¼ cup dry red wine
¼ cup finely chopped onion
4 (4- to 6-ounce) beef tenderloin steaks, about 1 inch thick

Squeeze roasted garlic pulp from skins; coarsely chop pulp. In small saucepan, over high heat, bring garlic, ½ cup steak sauce, wine and onion to a boil; reduce heat. Simmer 5 minutes; keep warm.

Grill steaks over medium heat or broil 6 inches from heat source 5 minutes on each side or to desired doneness, basting occasionally with remaining steak sauce. Serve steaks with warm sauce. Garnish as desired.

Makes 4 servings

Tenderloin with Roasted Garlic Sauce

Grilled Chili-Marinated Pork

3 tablespoons ground seeded dried pasilla chilies
1 teaspoon coarse or kosher salt
½ teaspoon ground cumin
2 tablespoons vegetable oil
1 tablespoon fresh lime juice
4 cloves garlic, minced
2 pounds pork tenderloin, trimmed of fat
Shredded romaine lettuce (optional)

Mix chilies, salt and cumin in small bowl. Stir in oil and lime juice to make smooth paste. Stir in garlic; set aside.

Butterfly pork by cutting lengthwise about ⅔ of the way through, being careful not to cut all the way through; spread meat flat. Cut tenderloin crosswise into 8 equal pieces. Place pork between pieces of plastic wrap. Pound with flat side of meat mallet to ¼-inch thickness. Spread chili paste on both sides of pork pieces to coat evenly. Place in shallow glass baking dish. Marinate, covered, in refrigerator 2 to 3 hours.

Prepare coals for grill or preheat broiler. Grill or broil pork 6 inches from heat 8 to 10 minutes for grilling or 6 to 7 minutes for broiling, turning once. Serve on lettuce-lined plate. Garnish, if desired. *Makes 6 to 8 servings*

Black Gold Burgers

¾ cup finely chopped onion
6 large cloves garlic, minced
2 tablespoons margarine
1 tablespoon sugar
¾ cup A.1. ORIGINAL® or A.1. BOLD® Steak Sauce
1½ pounds ground beef
6 onion rolls, split

In medium skillet, over medium heat, sauté onion and garlic in margarine until tender but not brown; stir in sugar. Reduce heat to low; cook 10 minutes more, stirring occasionally. Stir in steak sauce; keep warm.

Shape beef into 6 patties. Grill burgers over medium heat or broil 6 inches from heat source 5 minutes on each side or until no longer pink in center. Place burgers on roll bottoms; top each with 3 tablespoons warm sauce and roll top. Serve immediately.

Makes 6 servings

Grilled Chili-Marinated Pork

Spicy-Sweet Lamb Tagine with Saffron ■ Couscous ■

1 tablespoon olive oil
2 pounds boneless lamb shoulder or leg, cut into 1½- to 2-inch cubes
3 medium onions, cut into eighths
4 cloves garlic, minced
2 teaspoons ground ginger
2 teaspoons ground cinnamon
1 teaspoon black pepper
1 can (16 ounces) diced tomatoes, undrained
2 cups water
1 can (15 ounces) chick-peas, drained
1 cup chopped pitted prunes
½ teaspoon salt
1 small butternut squash, peeled, seeded and cut into 1-inch pieces
1 medium zucchini, halved and cut into 1-inch pieces
Saffron Couscous (page 77)
¼ cup chopped fresh cilantro or fresh parsley

Heat oil in Dutch oven over high heat. Add lamb in single layer. Cook, stirring occasionally, 7 to 10 minutes or until lamb is browned. Add onions, garlic, ginger, cinnamon and pepper; stir 30 seconds or until spices are fragrant. Add tomatoes and water. Scrape any browned bits from bottom of pan. Cover and bring to a boil. Reduce heat to medium-low and simmer 1 hour.

Remove 1 cup liquid from lamb mixture and place in medium saucepan. Continue simmering lamb, covered, 30 minutes, adding additional water, if needed. Add chick-peas, prunes and salt; simmer 20 minutes or until lamb is tender. Uncover and simmer until liquid is slightly thickened.

Add butternut squash to reserved liquid in medium saucepan. Cover and bring to a boil over high heat. Reduce heat to medium-low and simmer 20 minutes or until squash is tender. Add zucchini to butternut squash and simmer 10 to 15 minutes or until zucchini is tender. Set aside; cover to keep warm.

Prepare Saffron Couscous. Place on large serving platter. Form well in center of couscous. Spoon lamb stew in center; top with vegetables. Sprinkle with cilantro.

Makes 6 servings

Spicy-Sweet Lamb Tagine with Saffron Couscous

Saffron Couscous

2¼ cups water
1 tablespoon margarine or butter
¼ teaspoon salt
¼ teaspoon saffron threads, crushed *or* dash powdered saffron
10 ounces (1½ cups) quick-cooking couscous

Combine water, margarine, salt and saffron in medium saucepan. Bring to a boil over high heat. Stir in couscous. Cover; remove from heat. Let stand 5 minutes or until liquid is absorbed. Fluff couscous with fork. *Makes 6 servings*

Beef with ■ Dry Spice Rub ■

3 tablespoons firmly packed brown sugar
1 tablespoon black peppercorns
1 tablespoon yellow mustard seeds
1 tablespoon whole coriander seeds
4 cloves garlic
1½ to 2 pounds beef top round steak or London broil (about 1½ inches thick)
Vegetable or olive oil
Salt

Place sugar, peppercorns, seeds and garlic in blender or food processor; process until seeds and garlic are crushed. Rub beef with oil, then pat on spice mixture. Season to taste with salt. To prevent sticking, spray grid with nonstick cooking spray. Prepare coals for grilling. Grill beef, on covered grill, over medium-low KINGSFORD® briquets, 16 to 20 minutes for medium doneness, turning once. Let stand 5 minutes before slicing. Cut across grain into thin diagonal slices. Garnish, if desired. *Makes 6 servings*

Stuffed Smothered ■ Steak ■

4 cups sliced onions
2 tablespoons vegetable oil
¼ cup sliced garlic
¾ cup A.1. THICK & HEARTY® Steak Sauce, divided
1 (2-pound) beef top round steak, about 1½ inches thick

In large skillet, over medium heat, sauté onions in oil 8 to 10 minutes. Add garlic; cook 8 to 10 minutes more or until onions and garlic are soft and golden brown, stirring occasionally. Stir in ½ cup steak sauce; heat through. Set aside.

With sharp knife, make a horizontal pocket in side of steak, being careful not to cut all the way through. Stuff reserved onion mixture into pocket; secure with wooden toothpicks. Grill steak over medium heat or broil 6 inches from heat source 10 to 12 minutes on each side or to desired doneness, basting frequently with remaining ¼ cup steak sauce. Remove toothpicks; let steak rest 10 minutes. Slice steak. Serve immediately. *Makes 6 servings*

Beef with Dry Spice Rub

Lamb Brochettes with ■ Plums ■

2 tablespoons minced fresh cilantro
2 tablespoons olive oil
1 tablespoon lemon juice
3 teaspoons cumin, divided
5 medium garlic cloves, minced
1½ teaspoons salt, divided
1 teaspoon curry powder
¼ teaspoon ground red pepper
¼ teaspoon black pepper
1½ pounds leg of lamb, trimmed, cut into 1-inch cubes
8 fresh California plums, cut into wedges

To prepare marinade, combine cilantro, olive oil, lemon juice, 2 teaspoons cumin, garlic, 1 teaspoon salt, curry powder, red pepper and black pepper in large nonreactive bowl. Add lamb and toss well. Cover with plastic wrap; marinate lamb in refrigerator for 2 hours or overnight. Drain lamb; reserve marinade.

Starting with lamb, alternately thread 4 lamb cubes and 4 plum wedges onto metal skewers.* Brush with reserved marinade; sprinkle with remaining 1 teaspoon cumin and remaining ½ teaspoon salt.

Prepare coals for grilling or preheat broiler and cook, turning skewers occasionally, until lamb is medium-rare, 8 to 10 minutes. Transfer the brochettes to a serving platter or individual plates.

Makes 6 servings (2 kabobs each)

**If using bamboo skewers, soak in cold water 10 to 15 minutes to prevent burning.*

Favorite Recipe from **California Tree Fruit Agreement**

Pork Chops in ■ Creamy Garlic Sauce ■

1 cup chicken broth
¼ cup garlic cloves, peeled and crushed (about 12 to 15)
½ teaspoon olive oil
4 boneless pork loin chops, about ¼ inch thick each
1 tablespoon minced fresh parsley
½ teaspoon dried tarragon leaves
¼ teaspoon salt
¼ teaspoon black pepper
1 tablespoon all-purpose flour
2 tablespoons water
1 tablespoon dry sherry
2 cups cooked white rice

1. Place chicken broth and garlic in small saucepan. Bring to a boil over high heat. Cover; reduce heat to low. Simmer 25 to 30 minutes or until garlic mashes easily with fork. Set aside to cool. Process in blender or food processor until smooth.

2. Heat olive oil in large nonstick skillet over medium-high heat. Add pork; cook 1 to 1½ minutes on each side or until browned. Pour garlic mixture into skillet. Sprinkle with parsley, tarragon, salt and pepper. Bring to a boil; cover. Reduce heat to low; simmer 10 to 15 minutes or until pork is juicy and barely pink in center. Remove pork from skillet; keep warm.

3. Combine flour and water in small cup. Slowly pour flour mixture into skillet; bring to a boil. Cook and stir until mixture thickens. Stir in sherry. Serve sauce over pork and rice. Garnish as desired. *Makes 4 servings*

Pork Chops in Creamy Garlic Sauce

Tuscan-Style Lamb with White Beans

- 1 pound large dried lima (butter) beans
- 1 teaspoon olive oil
- 3 pounds lamb shoulder, cut into large pieces (fat trimmed)
- 3 onions, peeled and quartered
- 2 carrots, peeled and quartered
- 12 large cloves garlic, sliced
- 1 cup dry vermouth or red or white wine* (optional)
- 3 cups chicken broth
- 1 cup chopped celery, with leaves
- 2 bay leaves
- 2 large sprigs rosemary *or* 1 tablespoon dried rosemary, crumbled
- 1 to 2 cups (4 to 8 ounces) shredded JARLSBERG Cheese

**Note: If not using vermouth or wine, increase chicken broth to 4 cups.*

Rinse beans; place in large saucepan. Cover with 2 inches water. Bring to a boil over high heat; boil 2 minutes. Remove from heat; cover and let soak 1 hour. Drain beans; discard water. (Or soak beans in cold water overnight, drain and discard water.)

Heat oil in Dutch oven over high heat. Add lamb; cook and stir 10 minutes. Add onions, carrots and garlic; cook and stir 8 minutes, lifting lamb off bottom of pan to let vegetables cook.

Add vermouth, if desired, and cook 3 minutes. Add broth, celery, bay leaves and rosemary; cover and simmer 1½ hours. Add beans and shredded Jarlsberg and continue to simmer 40 minutes to 1 hour until beans are desired firmness. Remove bay leaves and discard before serving. *Makes 8 servings*

Tuscan-Style Lamb with White Beans

Lemon-Garlic Shish ■ Kabobs ■

- 1½ pounds well-trimmed boneless leg of lamb, cut into 1¼-inch pieces
- ¼ cup olive oil
- 2 tablespoons lemon juice
- 4 cloves garlic, minced
- 2 tablespoons chopped fresh oregano *or* 2 teaspoons dried oregano leaves
- ½ teaspoon salt
- ½ teaspoon black pepper
- 1 red or yellow bell pepper, cut into wedges
- 1 small zucchini, cut into 1-inch pieces
- 1 yellow squash, cut into 1-inch pieces
- 1 small red onion, cut into ½-inch wedges
- 8 ounces large fresh button mushrooms, stems trimmed
- Fresh oregano sprigs for garnish

Place lamb in large resealable plastic food storage bag. To prepare marinade, combine oil, juice, garlic, oregano, salt and black pepper in small bowl; pour marinade over lamb in bag. Seal bag tightly; turn to coat. Marinate lamb in refrigerator 1 to 4 hours, turning once.

To prevent sticking, spray grid with nonstick cooking spray. Prepare coals for grilling. Drain lamb; reserve marinade. Alternately thread lamb, bell pepper, zucchini, yellow squash, onion and mushrooms onto 12 (10-inch) metal skewers;* brush both sides with reserved marinade.

Grill kabobs, on covered grill, over medium-hot coals 6 minutes. Turn; continue to grill, covered, 5 to 7 minutes for medium or until desired doneness is reached. Garnish, if desired.

Makes 6 servings (2 kabobs each)

**If using bamboo skewers, soak in cold water 10 to 15 minutes to prevent burning.*

Lemon-Garlic Shish Kabobs

■ Fajitas ■

½ cup lime juice *or* ¼ cup lime juice and ¼ cup tequila or beer
1 tablespoon minced garlic
1 tablespoon dried oregano leaves
2 teaspoons ground cumin
2 teaspoons black pepper
1 pound flank steak
6 (10-inch) flour tortillas or 12 (7-inch) flour tortillas
4 bell peppers, any color, halved
1 large bunch green onions
Salsa Cruda (page 13)
1 cup coarsely chopped fresh cilantro
1 ripe avocado, thinly sliced
6 tablespoons sour cream

1. To prepare marinade, combine lime juice, garlic, oregano, cumin and black pepper in small bowl. Place flank steak in resealable plastic food storage bag; pour marinade over steak. Press air from bag and seal; turn bag to coat. Refrigerate 30 minutes or up to 24 hours.

2. Place tortillas in stacks of 3. Wrap each stack in foil; set aside.

3. Drain marinade from meat into small saucepan. Bring to a boil over high heat. Remove from heat; set aside.

4. To prevent sticking, spray grid with nonstick cooking spray. Adjust grid 4 to 6 inches above heat. Prepare coals for grilling. Place meat in center of grill over medium-hot coals. Place bell peppers, skin side down, around meat; cover. Grill peppers 6 minutes or until skin is spotted with brown. Turn over and continue grilling 6 to 8 minutes or until tender. Move to sides of grill to keep warm while meat finishes grilling.

5. Grill meat, basting frequently with marinade, 8 minutes or until brown. Turn; grill 8 to 10 minutes or until slightly pink in center for medium doneness. During the last 4 minutes of grilling, brush onions with remaining marinade; grill 1 to 2 minutes. Turn; grill 1 to 2 minutes more or until tender.

6. Place wrapped packets of tortillas on grill; heat about 5 minutes. Slice peppers and onions into thin 2-inch-long strips. Thinly slice meat across the grain.

7. Place tortilla on plate. Place meat, peppers, onions, Salsa Cruda and cilantro in center of each tortilla. Fold sides completely over filling to enclose. Serve with avocado and sour cream.

Makes 6 servings

Fajitas

Provençal-Style Lamb ■ Shanks ■

- **2 tablespoons olive oil**
- **4 lamb shanks (about 1 pound each)**
- **2 large onions, chopped**
- **5 cloves garlic, minced, divided**
- **1 can (28 ounces) Italian-style plum tomatoes, undrained and coarsely chopped**
- **½ cup dry vermouth**
- **1½ teaspoons dried basil leaves**
- **1½ teaspoons dried rosemary**
- **1 teaspoon salt**
- **½ teaspoon black pepper**
- **1 can (19 ounces) cannellini beans, rinsed and drained**
- **1½ tablespoons balsamic vinegar (optional)**
- **2 tablespoons chopped fresh Italian parsley**
- **1 teaspoon grated lemon peel**

Heat 1 tablespoon oil in Dutch oven over medium heat; add 2 lamb shanks. Brown on all sides; transfer to large plate with tongs. Repeat with remaining 1 tablespoon oil and 2 lamb shanks.

Add onions and 4 cloves garlic to drippings in Dutch oven; cook 6 to 8 minutes until onions are tender, stirring occasionally. Add tomatoes with liquid, vermouth, basil, rosemary, salt and pepper; bring to a boil over medium-high heat. Return shanks to Dutch oven. Reduce heat to low; cover and simmer 1½ hours or until shanks are tender.

Remove shanks; cool slightly. Skim fat from pan juices with large spoon; discard. Stir beans into pan juices; heat through. Cut lamb from shanks into 1-inch pieces; discard bones and gristle. Return lamb to Dutch oven; heat through. Stir in vinegar.

Combine parsley, lemon peel and remaining clove garlic in small bowl. To serve, ladle lamb mixture into 6 individual shallow serving bowls; sprinkle with parsley mixture. Garnish, if desired.

Makes 6 servings

Provençal-Style Lamb Shanks

Grilled Pork and Potatoes Vesuvio

1 center-cut boneless pork loin roast (1½ pounds), well trimmed
½ cup dry white wine
2 tablespoons olive oil
4 cloves garlic, minced, divided
1½ to 2 pounds small red potatoes (about 1½ inches in diameter), scrubbed
12 lemon wedges
Salt and black pepper
¼ cup chopped fresh parsley
1 teaspoon finely grated lemon peel

Cut pork into 1-inch cubes. Place pork in large resealable plastic food storage bag. To prepare marinade, combine wine, oil and 3 cloves minced garlic in small bowl; pour marinade over pork.

Place potatoes in single layer in microwavable dish. Pierce each potato with tip of sharp knife. Microwave at HIGH 6 to 7 minutes or until almost tender when pierced with fork. (Or, place potatoes in large saucepan. Cover with cold water. Bring to a boil over high heat. Simmer about 12 minutes or until almost tender when pierced with fork.) Immediately rinse potatoes with cold water to cool; drain.

Add to pork in bag. Seal bag tightly; turn to coat. Marinate in refrigerator at least 2 hours or up to 8 hours, turning occasionally.

To prevent sticking, spray grid with nonstick cooking spray. Prepare coals for grilling. Drain pork mixture; discard marinade. Alternately thread about 3 pork cubes and 2 potatoes onto 12 (10-inch) metal skewers.* Place 1 lemon wedge on end of each skewer. Sprinkle salt and pepper over pork and potatoes.

Grill skewers, on covered grill, over medium coals 14 to 16 minutes or until pork is juicy and barely pink in center and potatoes are tender, turning halfway through grilling time.

Remove skewers from grill. Combine parsley, lemon peel and remaining minced garlic clove in small bowl. Sprinkle over pork and potatoes. Squeeze lemon wedges over pork and potatoes.

Makes 6 servings

**If using bamboo skewers, soak in cold water 10 to 15 minutes to prevent burning.*

Grilled Pork and Potatoes Vesuvio

Acknowledgments

The publishers would like to thank the companies and organizations listed below for the use of their recipes and photos in this publication.

California Tree Fruit Agreement

Christopher Ranch Garlic

Filippo Berio Olive Oil

Lipton

McIlhenny Company

Nabisco, Inc.

National Pasta Association

National Turkey Federation

Newman's Own, Inc.®

Norseland, Inc.

North Dakota Beef Commission

Perdue® Farms

Sonoma Dried Tomato

StarKist® Seafood Company

Index

Albacore Salad Puttanesca with Garlic Vinaigrette, 18
Appetizers
Elephant in a Bowl, 14
Fiery Garlic Bagel Thins, 12
Garlic Bites, 11
Garlic Fritters, 12
Herbed Garlic Cheese Spread, 10
Marshall's Garlic Popcorn, 10
Roasted Eggplant Dip, 8
Roasted Garlic Hummus, 12
Salsa Cruda, 13
Stuffed Mushrooms, 13
Venezuelan Salsa, 14

Baked Chicken with Crispy Cheese-Garlic Crust, 60
Baked Rockfish Veracruz, 64
Baked Shrimp with Chili-Garlic Butter, 62
Baked Tortilla Strips, 21
Balsamic-Herb Vinaigrette, 34
Beans
Chili Verde, 24
Hearty Cassoulet, 48
Layered Mexican Salad, 22
Provençal-Style Lamb Shanks, 88
Roasted Garlic Hummus, 12
Spicy-Sweet Lamb Tagine with Saffron Couscous, 76
Tuscan-Style Lamb with White Beans, 82
Beef
Beef with Dry Spice Rub, 78
Black Gold Burgers, 74
Fajitas, 86
Stuffed Smothered Steak, 78
Tenderloins with Roasted Garlic Sauce, 72
Beef with Dry Spice Rub, 78
Black Gold Burgers, 74

Casseroles
Crab and Corn Enchilada Casserole, 66
Hearty Cassoulet, 48
Turkey & Zucchini Enchiladas with Tomatillo-Green Chili Sauce, 56
Cheese
Baked Chicken with Crispy Cheese-Garlic Crust, 60
Chili-Crusted Grilled Chicken Caesar Salad, 26
Crab and Corn Enchilada Casserole, 66
Elephant in a Bowl, 14
Focaccia with Dried Tomatoes and Fontina, 32
Garlic Fritters, 12
Herbed Garlic Cheese Spread, 10
Layered Mexican Salad, 22
Orzo with Spinach and Red Pepper, 38
Parmesan Polenta, 36
Pasta Twists with Spinach Pesto, 42
Stuffed Jumbo Shells with Garlic Vegetables, 40
Stuffed Mushrooms, 13
Sweet Pepper Garlic Soup, 16
Turkey & Zucchini Enchiladas with Tomatillo-Green Chili Sauce, 56
Tuscan-Style Lamb with White Beans, 82
Chicken Breasts
Chili-Crusted Grilled Chicken Caesar Salad, 26
Garlicky Chicken Packets, 61
Jamaican Rum Chicken, 52
Spicy Island Chicken, 50
Chicken Pieces
Baked Chicken with Crispy Cheese-Garlic Crust, 60
Forty Clove Chicken, 59
Chicken Thighs
Garlic Chicken and Corn Stir-Fry, 60
Ginger Hot Thighs, 59
Hearty Cassoulet, 48
Chili-Crusted Grilled Chicken Caesar Salad, 26
Chili Verde, 24
Crab and Corn Enchilada Casserole, 66

Elephant in a Bowl, 14

Fajitas, 86
Far East Tabbouleh, 22
Fiery Garlic Bagel Thins, 12
Fish
Albacore Salad Puttanesca with Garlic Vinaigrette, 18
Baked Rockfish Veracruz, 64
Fish Fantastic and Fast, 68
Fish Stock, 70
Seafood Paella, 70
Fish Fantastic and Fast, 68
Focaccia with Dried Tomatoes and Fontina, 32
Forty Clove Chicken, 59
French Pan-Roasted Hens, 54
Fruit
Lamb Brochettes with Plums, 80
Spicy-Sweet Lamb Tagine with Saffron Couscous, 76
Taos Tossed Salad, 21
Venezuelan Salsa, 14

Garlic Bites, 11
Garlic Chicken and Corn Stir-Fry, 60
Garlic Clams, 68
Garlic Fritters, 12
Garlicky Chicken Packets, 61
Garlic Shrimp with Noodles, 42
Garlic Stir-Fry, 30
Garlic Vegetables, 40
Garlic Vinaigrette Dressing, 18
Gilroy Garlic Soup, 24
Ginger Hot Thighs, 59
Grilled Balsamic-Herb Ratatouille, 34
Grilled Chili-Marinated Pork, 74
Grilled Pork and Potatoes Vesuvio, 90
Grilled Summer Gazpacho, 20

Hearty Cassoulet, 48
Herbed Garlic Cheese Spread, 10

Jamaican Rum Chicken, 52
Jen's Ginger-Garlic Chicken Drummettes, 61

Lamb
Lamb Brochettes with Plums, 80
Lemon-Garlic Shish Kabobs, 84
Provençal-Style Lamb Shanks, 88
Spicy-Sweet Lamb Tagine with Saffron Couscous, 76
Tuscan-Style Lamb with White Beans, 82
Layered Mexican Salad, 22
Lemon-Garlic Broccoli over Spaghetti Squash, 30
Lemon Garlic Greens, 36
Lemon-Garlic Grilling Sauce, 64
Lemon-Garlic Shish Kabobs, 84

Marshall's Garlic Popcorn, 10
Mexican Tortilla Soup, 18

Index

Orzo with Spinach and Red Pepper, 38

Parmesan Polenta, 36
Pasta
Albacore Salad Puttanesca with Garlic Vinaigrette, 18
Garlic Shrimp with Noodles, 42
Orzo with Spinach and Red Pepper, 38
Pasta Twists with Spinach Pesto, 42
Pasta with Zucchini and Roasted Garlic, 44
Saffron Couscous, 77
Spinach Fettuccine with Garlic-Onion Sauce, 44
Stuffed Jumbo Shells with Garlic Vegetables, 40
Summer Garden Harvest Fusilli, 46
Thailand Peanut Pesto, 46
Pasta Twists with Spinach Pesto, 42
Pasta with Zucchini and Roasted Garlic, 44
Pork
Chili Verde, 24
Grilled Chili-Marinated Pork, 74
Grilled Pork and Potatoes Vesuvio, 90
Pork Chops in Creamy Garlic Sauce, 80
Pork Chops in Creamy Garlic Sauce, 80
Provençal-Style Lamb Shanks, 88

Rice
Baked Rockfish Veracruz, 64
Garlic Chicken and Corn Stir-Fry, 60
Pork Chops in Creamy Garlic Sauce, 80
Seafood Paella, 70
Turkey Breast Braised with Garlic and Rice, 58
Turkey Jambalaya, 54
Roasted Chicken and Veggies, 55
Roasted Eggplant Dip, 8
Roasted Garlic
Forty Clove Chicken, 59
Herbed Garlic Cheese Spread, 10
Pasta with Zucchini and Roasted Garlic, 44
Roasted Garlic Hummus, 12
Rosemary-Garlic Mashed Potatoes, 28
Tenderloins with Roasted Garlic Sauce, 72
Turkey Breast Braised with Garlic and Rice, 58
Roasted Garlic Hummus, 12
Rosemary-Garlic Mashed Potatoes, 28

Saffron Couscous, 77
Salads
Albacore Salad Puttanesca with Garlic Vinaigrette, 18
Chili-Crusted Grilled Chicken Caesar Salad, 26
Far East Tabbouleh, 22
Layered Mexican Salad, 22
Taos Tossed Salad, 21
Salsa Cruda, 13
Sauces
Lemon-Garlic Grilling Sauce, 64
Salsa Cruda, 13
Spicy Tomato Sauce, 67
Tomatillo-Green Chili Sauce, 57
Venezuelan Salsa, 14
Sautéed Garlic Potatoes, 32
Seafood
Baked Shrimp with Chili-Garlic Butter, 62
Crab and Corn Enchilada Casserole, 66
Garlic Clams, 68
Seafood Paella, 70
Shrimp Scampi, 67
Seafood Paella, 70
Shrimp Scampi, 67
Side Dishes
Focaccia with Dried Tomatoes and Fontina, 32
Parmesan Polenta, 36
Rosemary-Garlic Mashed Potatoes, 28
Sautéed Garlic Potatoes, 32
Soups
Chili Verde, 24
Gilroy Garlic Soup, 24
Grilled Summer Gazpacho, 20
Mexican Tortilla Soup, 18
Sweet Pepper Garlic Soup, 16
Spicy Island Chicken, 50
Spicy-Sweet Lamb Tagine with Saffron Couscous, 76
Spicy Tomato Sauce, 67
Spinach Fettuccine with Garlic-Onion Sauce, 44
Stuffed Jumbo Shells with Garlic Vegetables, 40
Stuffed Mushrooms, 13
Stuffed Smothered Steak, 78
Summer Garden Harvest Fusilli, 46
Sweet Pepper Garlic Soup, 16

Taos Tossed Salad, 21
Tenderloins with Roasted Garlic Sauce, 72
Thailand Peanut Pesto, 46
Tomatillo-Green Chili Sauce, 57
Turkey
Hearty Cassoulet, 48
Turkey & Zucchini Enchiladas with Tomatillo-Green Chili Sauce, 56
Turkey Breast Braised with Garlic and Rice, 58
Turkey Jambalaya, 54
Turkey & Zucchini Enchiladas with Tomatillo-Green Chili Sauce, 56
Turkey Breast Braised with Garlic and Rice, 58
Turkey Jambalaya, 54
Tuscan-Style Lamb with White Beans, 82

Venezuelan Salsa, 14